Inspiring Words
FROM THE PSALMS
FOR MOMS

Nana Talley
Presented to

Ashleigh Riddle
Presented by

May 9:05
Date

Inspiring Words

FROM THE PSALMS

FOR MOMS

Blue Sky Ink
Brentwood, Tennessee

Inspiring Words from the Psalms for Moms
Copyright © 2004 by GRQ, Inc.
ISBN 1-59475-001-7

Published by Blue Sky Ink,
Brentwood, Tennesse

Compiler and Editor: Lila Empson
Writer: P. Barnhart
Cover and Text Design: Diane Whisner

Upon you I have leaned from my birth;
it was you who took me from my mother's womb.
My praise is continually of you.

PSALM 71:6 NRSV

Contents

Introduction

She was in the backseat holding her young son when the car hit a patch of ice and spun out of control. The driver fiercely battled the swerving car, but it began rolling off the road. Having already squeezed her arms tightly around her child, the mother planted her

feet on the floor and braced her shoulder against the window as the car toppled over again and again. Finally all movement stopped, and the car came to rest against a hillside. The mother was quietly speaking the last of a prayer she had begun when the car began its slide. The child was not seriously injured. His mother's embrace had saved him.

The saving embrace of a mother is a gift from God. In the book of Psalms, also a gift from God, there is guidance for moms. There are encouragement and strength for them to write on the hearts of their children what nothing can erase.

Let all who take refuge in you rejoice;
let them ever sing for joy.
Spread your protection over them,
so that those who love your name
may exult in you.
For you bless the righteous,
O LORD;
you cover them with favor as with a shield.

PSALM 5:11–12 NRSV

God Loves a Mother's Prayer

They find joy in obeying the Law of the LORD, and they study it day and night. They are like trees that grow beside a stream, that bear fruit at the right time, and whose leaves do not dry up. They succeed in everything they do.

PSALM 1:2–3 GNT

Like most mothers, you're probably a great prayer-maker. One look at your children as they leave for school, play with their friends in the front yard, or open birthday presents can bring a prayer to your lips. You pray for your children's protection, give thanks for their joy, and beg God to guide them as they grow. You ask God to help you be a good mom. God loves a mother's prayer, and you find yourself talking often with God because your children are so precious. You want God to hold your children in the palm of his hand.

God has so much to say to you when you listen with your heart. God tells you to have faith in his goodness, not to worry. God tells you that he loves your children even more than you do. God promises to work through you as you raise your children the best you can.

You can pray to God today because God listens to your prayers.

I cried unto the
LORD with my
voice, and he
heard me out of
his holy hill.

PSALM 3:4 KJV

God Is Your Shield

You, O LORD, are a shield around me,
my glory, and the one who lifts up my head.
PSALM 3:3 NRSV

As a mom, you have a special job—to protect your children so that they can grow up healthy and happy. You make sure they eat a balanced diet and brush their teeth, take them to the doctor for regular checkups, hold their hands when they cross the street, and make sure they wear their raincoats in the rain.

You call on God to protect your children, to shield them with the brightness of his light, to hide them in the shadow of his wings. Praying for God's protection is as important as making sure that your children have their seat belts fastened. God covers your children with his goodness and mercy.

God is your shield too. God watches over you and helps you to raise healthy, happy children. God's shield is very big—it covers you and your children as surely as a warm, downy blanket on a cold winter's night.

You can relax today knowing that God is your shield.

God's my island hideaway,
keeps danger far from the
shore, throws garlands of
hosannas around my neck.

PSALM 32:7 THE MESSAGE

Love Watches Over You

*I sleep and wake up refreshed
because you, LORD, protect me.*
PSALM 3:5 CEV

Another busy day. Carpool in the morning. A soccer match and a swim meet in the afternoon. Dinner to cook. Homework to supervise. Through all the activity, God's love watches over you and your kids.

Because God's love watches over you, you can go about the business of raising your children free from worry or anxiety. No matter how busy you are, God's love, like the air you breathe, sustains you. God's love wraps about you, like a comfy, well-worn sweater. No matter what you do, you can count on the power of God's love watching over you to make everything all right. No matter where you go, the love of God follows you and gives you the strength you need to be a good mom.

God's first words to you in the morning are *I love you,* and God's last words to you at night are *I love you.* With love like that, you can do anything.

The power of God's love is with you now.

I trust in your love. My heart is happy because you saved me.

PSALM 13:5 NCV

Mornings with God

I will sing of your might; I will sing aloud of your steadfast love in the morning. For you have been a fortress for me and a refuge in the day of my distress.

PSALM 59:16 NRSV

Mornings are not necessarily the most peaceful time of the day, especially on school days. You have to get the kids out of bed and into clothes, put a little breakfast into them and supervise teeth brushing, pack and distribute lunches. When you finally get the kids off to school, it's your turn to get ready for your work.

Thank God for weekends! You can get up a little early on a Saturday before the whole house wakes up, make a cup of tea, wrap up in a throw on the couch, and have a good talk with God. Saturday mornings are a good time to ask God for what you need. You spend the rest of the week making sure your family has what they need. Now it's your turn. When you sit quietly on the couch and listen carefully, your heart will tell you what you need from God.

God listens carefully to hear what it is you want from him.

Inspiring Words FROM THE PSALMS

O LORD, You have heard
the desire of the humble;
You will strengthen their heart,
You will incline Your ear.

PSALM 10:17 NASB

The Wonder of God

*Here I am, your invited guest—it's incredible! I enter
your house; here I am, prostrate in your inner sanctum.*
PSALM 5:7 THE MESSAGE

Every mother has experienced the power of wonder. When your
babies were born, you were overwhelmed by wonder. As your babes were laid in your arms for the first time, the wonder and awe of each little baby dissolved you in tears of joy to see what God had created.

Your babies may be children now, or teenagers or grownups with families of their own, but you still experience the wonder of God in the miracle of their lives. Whenever you look carefully at your children, whether they're tiny tots or grownups, you can see God's handiwork in them. When you see how God is at work in their lives, your wonder at the goodness of God can be overwhelming. You are reminded of the first time you held them close, and you experience again the wonder and joy of seeing what God has created.

*You can look carefully at your children
and know the wonder of God.*

From everlasting to everlasting, the LORD's mercy is on those who fear him. His righteousness belongs to their children and grandchildren.

PSALM 103:17 GOD'S WORD

God's Children

You have made them a little lower than God, and
crowned them with glory and honor.

PSALM 8:5 NRSV

As a mother, you know that underneath the dirt and scruffiness from the playground, and behind their mischievousness and unwillingness to clean their plates at dinner, your children seem like angels. When you see your children peacefully sound asleep, you have no doubt that your children do indeed have heavenly origins.

Your children are God's children—and so are you, their mother. For you, too, are a special creature among all God's creation. You are God's child, loved best and most by God. God has marked you as his own, and he has crowned you with honor and glory. Like the angels in heaven, you shine with the love of God, your Father.

Now God has trusted you to raise and love and protect your children. He has trusted their well-being to you. You take care of your children with a fierce mother's love that shines brighter and stronger than the sun at noonday.

You are bright and shining, touched by God's love.

*Y*ou created my inmost
being; you knit me together
in my mother's womb.

PSALM 139:13 NIV

Bountiful Gifts

I will sing unto the LORD, because he
hath dealt bountifully with me.
PSALM 13:6 KJV

Love is your greatest characteristic as a mother, but the next greatest feature you have is your unlimited ability to give. You are a natural giver. Love inspires all your gifts to your children. Of course, you give your children the basic necessities of life—food, clothing, and shelter; you give them education; medical care. You also give limitless time and attention to help them grow into good and loving adults. You make sure they learn about God and his ways, and how much God loves them.

Just as you give good gifts to your children, God gives good gifts to you. God blesses you every moment of every day with faith and courage to raise your children well. God touches you with his mercy and forgiveness so that when you make mistakes, you can try again—and you do. God wraps you in his love, which you give freely to your children.

God gives you gifts every moment today.

O LORD my God, you have done many miracles for us. Your plans for us are too numerous to list. If I tried to recite all your wonderful deeds, I would never come to the end of them.

PSALM 40:5 NLT

A Mother's Way

*LORD, who may abide in Your tabernacle? Who may
dwell in Your holy hill? He who walks uprightly, and
works righteousness, and speaks the truth in his heart.*

PSALM 15:1–2 NKJV

It's been said that imitation is the highest form of flattery.

Children love to imitate their mothers.
Whether they are playing house or mim-
icking your conversation, children practice
at being grownups by pretending they are
the mom. Children naturally want to follow their mothers wherever they go, what-
ever they do. As a mother, you show your
children the way through life.

Part of your job is to show your children how to live so that they
can follow you into happy adulthood. You speak truthfully to your
children and show them by your actions how much God loves them.
This is a mother's way—to "imitate" God's love. When you speak
and live God's love, your children naturally want to follow you and
be like you. You seek to raise your children to be merciful, wise, and
loving grownups.

*Today you travel a mother's way and show your
children how to follow God's way.*

I am constantly aware of
your unfailing love, and
I have lived according to
your truth.

PSALM 26:3 NLT

A Mother's Identity

I said to the LORD, "You are my Lord.
Without you, I have nothing good."
PSALM 16:2 GOD'S WORD

As a mother, you are many things. You are a lover, a caregiver, and a provider. You are a teacher, a referee, and a driver. You are an organizer, a cheerleader, and a champion. You are a meal planner, a grocery shopper, a cook, a dishwasher, a laundress, and a mender as well. You love being all those things because you love being a mom.

You have been touched by God's goodness. You have been chosen to be among a special group of God's people—mothers. God has planted a special kind of love in your heart. It is a love without end; it is a love that multiplies with each child. It is the love that marks you as God's chosen one. It is the love you freely share with your children whether today you're cooking short-order or driving carpool or supervising homework. You know deep in your heart how much God loves you.

You are a mother, chosen by God's love.

Because you are my help, I sing
in the shadow of your wings.
My soul clings to you; your
right hand upholds me.

PSALM 63:7–8 NIV

The Mothers Before You

The boundary lines have fallen for me in pleasant places; surely I have a delightful inheritance.
PSALM 16:6 NIV

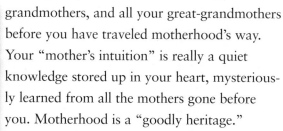

Motherhood is an ancient path you travel. Your mother, your grandmothers, and all your great-grandmothers before you have traveled motherhood's way. Your "mother's intuition" is really a quiet knowledge stored up in your heart, mysteriously learned from all the mothers gone before you. Motherhood is a "goodly heritage."

God has given you the heritage of motherhood. You are the heir of motherly love before you; and you are the steward of the motherly love that will come after you through your children. You are a link in a vast chain of God's own making, passing on from mother to child that which is good and loving and true. As a mother, you can be proud and humble at the same time for all you've inherited. You can be grateful to all of your women ancestors—the mothers who've handed you the torch of sacred motherhood.

You stand as a link in a long chain of motherly love, blessed and held together by God.

A posterity shall serve Him. It will be recounted of the LORD to the next generation, they will come and declare His righteousness to a people who will be born, that He has done this.

PSALM 22:30–31 NKJV

Motherhood's Solid Foundation

*I have set the LORD always before me; because He
is at my right hand I shall not be moved.*

PSALM 16:8 NKJV

You can pick up nearly any family-focused magazine today and find countless tips and guides to help you be a better mother. Teachers and mentors and leaders of various child-rearing techniques are everywhere, and they will always fill your world. As helpful as some of these guides may be, however, you can always turn to a more solid foundation.

God is your foundation. God is your ultimate guide in all things—especially the care of your children. God is big enough and strong enough to help you in all you ask and in all you seek to do. No fad or force on the planet can move you, because God walks with you at your right side every moment of every day. You can turn to God and open your heart, confident in God's mercy and love. You can place your precious children in God's gentle, loving hands.

*Your solid foundation is God, and he holds
you in the palm of his hand.*

May He send you help from the sanctuary and support you from Zion!

PSALM 20:2 NASB

Enjoying God

You have made known to me the path of life;
you will fill me with joy in your presence, with
eternal pleasures at your right hand.

PSALM 16:11 NIV

A lot of times, being a mother is fun. When you play with your

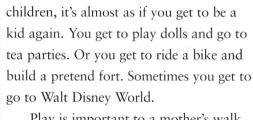

children, it's almost as if you get to be a kid again. You get to play dolls and go to tea parties. Or you get to ride a bike and build a pretend fort. Sometimes you get to go to Walt Disney World.

Play is important to a mother's walk with God, too. God enjoys you—and God wants you to enjoy him as well. God wants you to take pleasure in him. That

means you can have fun with God. You don't have to be serious all the time—you can bring God into your playtime with your kids; you can lie in a hammock and daydream with God; you can take a long walk with God and not talk about anything much at all. Your relationship with God is to be enjoyed. Do something with God just for the fun of it.

There is time today to enjoy God.

So that my soul may praise
you and not be silent.
O LORD my God, I will give
thanks to you forever.

PSALM 30:12 NRSV

A Mother's Prayer

I call upon you, for you will answer me, O God;
incline your ear to me, hear my words.

PSALM 17:6 NRSV

Moms spend a lot of time listening. When your children are young, you listen to their endless questions about how the world works and why it works the way it does. When your children are teenagers, you listen to them as they tell you all about their trials and tribulations at school, about their new boyfriends or girl-friends. When your children marry and have children of their own, you love to listen to stories about your grandchildren.

God spends a lot of time listening to mothers. God listens to you tell him how proud you are of your children. God listens to you when you ask for strength and help to be the best mother you can be. God listens to you as you place your precious children in his lov-ing arms. God loves to listen to a mother's prayer. Know that when-ever you call on God, he listens to every word you say.

God loves to listen to a mother's prayer.

I hope in You,
O LORD; You will
answer, O LORD
my God.

PSALM 38:15 NASB

The Love of God

"I love You, O Lord, my strength." The Lord is my rock and my fortress and my deliverer, my God, my rock, in whom I take refuge; my shield and the horn of my salvation, my stronghold.

PSALM 18:1–2 NASB

Everything about motherhood can be summed up in one word—*love*. Everything you do, everything you say, every ounce of your being, is motivated by love. Your giving, your patience, your compassion, your understanding, and your hope—in fact, all of motherhood's qualities—are rooted in the love you have for your children.

Similarly, everything about God can also be summed up in the same word—*love*. Yet as hard as it is to imagine, God's love for you is deeper, more powerful, and more all-knowing than even your love for your children. There is nothing you can do or think or say that can keep God from loving you. God follows you into the most secret places of your heart to tell you how much he loves you. You are God's child—and God loves you fiercely, deeply, and eternally.

God's love for you is so great that nothing in heaven or on earth can separate you from him.

*P*our out your unfailing love on those who love you; give justice to those with honest hearts.

PSALM 36:10 NLT

A Mother's Nightlight

Thou wilt light my candle: the LORD my
God will enlighten my darkness.
PSALM 18:28 KJV

"If you turn off the lights, it'll be dark, and the monsters in the closet will come out and get me!" What mother hasn't heard, at some time or other, a child's reason like this one for keeping a light on at bedtime? So you compromise—you turn out the main light in the room, but you turn on a nightlight to keep the monsters away. There's enough light to chase away the darkness.

Your faith in God is a mother's "nightlight." Unfortunately, you can't see into your children's futures—the way is dark and hidden from your view, but you can hope that your children's futures will be bright because you believe God loves them and holds them in the palm of his hand. It's okay that you can't see into your children's futures—because you know God, who is your lamp, is there ahead of you, lighting the way.

The light of God in your life makes
your children's futures bright.

You will help me, Lord God,
and keep me from falling.

PSALM 54:4 CEV

God's Glory

The heavens declare the glory of God;
the skies proclaim the work of his hands.
PSALM 19:1 NIV

*T*winkle, twinkle, little star" is one of the first tunes children learn to sing. Children seem naturally drawn to the stars; they love to look up at the heavens, their imaginations winging through time and space. Your children are constantly pointing you to the glory of God.

As a mother, you have a lot to teach your children, but your children have a lot to teach you as well. Maybe children can show the glory of God in the heavens because they have come so recently from God. Not yet set in adult ways, their minds are still fresh and full of God's glory. On a warm summer's evening, let your children take you by the hand and lead you out to the backyard. There you can look up at the soft night sky, full of stars, the handiwork of God. Let the children tell you stories of what they see there.

The glory of God shines over you. All
you have to do is look up.

The glory of the LORD shall endure for ever:
the LORD shall rejoice in his works.

PSALM 104:31 KJV

A Mother's Powerful Words

Let the words of my mouth
and the meditation of my heart
be acceptable in Your sight,
O LORD, my rock and my Redeemer.
PSALM 19:14 NASB

A mother's words are very powerful. Your words instruct your children, telling them right from wrong. Your words communicate your deep love and caring. Your words correct your children when they've misbehaved. Your words guide them through the troubles and triumphs of their days. As a mother, your words have a tremendous impact on the shape of your children's lives and spirits.

Your words are powerful in another way as well. Your words also have a tremendous impact on God. God listens carefully and is influenced by what you say. So you must choose your words carefully. Your prayers to God should always be said with love and honor and wonder—and they should always end in gratitude for the blessings of this life. You want the words of your mouth to be pleasing and acceptable to God, who loves you and wants to give you his very best.

May the words of your mouth be acceptable to God today.

I entreated Your favor
with my whole heart;
be merciful to me
according to Your word.

PSALM 119:58 NKJV

Your Heart's Desire

May he give you the desire of your heart
and make all your plans succeed.
PSALM 20:4 NIV

You want the best of everything for your children. You naturally want your kids to have the best homes, the best clothes, the best schools. You want them to have the brightest futures. You want them to be successful in work and in life. So far as it is within your power, you want to give them the desires of their hearts.

You are God's child. God naturally wants you to have the very best of everything life has to offer. Even more, God longs to give you your heart's deepest desire. What does your heart desire the most? If you look long and hard and deeply into the most secret place of your heart, you will find this simple desire: You want God. You want your children to want God more than anything in the world. It is this desire above all others that God is delighted to grant.

May God grant all your desires
and fulfill all your plans.

I truly believe I will live to
see the LORD's goodness.
PSALM 27:13 NCV

The Great Shepherd

The LORD is my shepherd; I shall not want.
He makes me to lie down in green pastures;
He leads me beside the still waters.

PSALM 23:1–2 NKJV

A mother's job, of course, is to take care of her children. So you spend most of your time as a caregiver. It's a rewarding, fulfilling

job—but it can also be tiring. You need to be taken care of too if you're to continue to give the best of yourself.

God, the Great Shepherd, is a mother's caregiver. The Great Shepherd takes care of you by giving you direction in your life. He walks beside you every day, leading and guiding you gently in the way you should go. He provides for you. He gives you what you need spiritually every day, leading you to still waters and soft green pastures to restore your soul.

All the Great Shepherd needs from you is a willingness to follow him. You only need to trust him, one step at a time, to take care of you every moment of every day.

Today you can follow God with
an open and willing heart.

I look up to the hills, but where does my help come from? My help comes from the LORD, who made heaven and earth. He will not let you be defeated. He who guards you never sleeps.

PSALM 121:1–3 NCV

God's Hands

The earth and everything on it belong to the LORD.
The world and its people belong to him.
PSALM 24:1 CEV

"He's got the whole world in His hands," the children sing in Sunday school. Straight from the mouths of babes comes this simple truth—that God, the Creator of this beautiful planet and all the stars above, is in control. God is in control of the great universe—and God is in control of everyone's life.

For you as a mother, this truth comes as a great relief. What freedom this is! Because God's got the whole world in his hands, you can let God do his job and you are free to do your job. You don't have to be in total control all the time—you can relax knowing that your life and the lives of your children are in God's capable hands. Since you don't have to be in total control, all you have to do is be responsible and do the very best you can—you can leave the rest to God.

You can relax today because God's
got the whole world in his hands.

O Lord, you have been our refuge throughout every generation. Before the mountains were born, before you gave birth to the earth and the world, you were God. You are God from everlasting to everlasting.

PSALM 90:1–2 GOD'S WORD

God, Your Teacher

Show me your ways, O LORD, teach me your paths;
guide me in your truth and teach me, for you are
God my Savior, and my hope is in you all day long.
PSALM 25:4–5 NIV

As a mother, you teach your children, but you do much more than help them with their homework. You teach what kids can't get out of a textbook or a classroom. You have the responsibility to teach your children right from wrong. You have the privilege to show your children how to love God, how to love themselves, and how to love others. Where do you go to get this heartfelt knowledge?

You turn to God and God's word in the Bible. You humbly ask God to instruct your heart in his way and truth. From God and the Bible you learn right from wrong, and you learn how to love God, yourself, and others. You pass that knowledge on to your children. For when you teach the way of God, you give your children a gift more precious than mere book knowledge—you give them the gift of how to live a happy life at peace with God.

God will teach you his way and truth today.

You are my God. Show me what you want me to do, and let your gentle Spirit lead me in the right path.

PSALM 143:10 CEV

God's House

*O LORD, I love the house in which you dwell, and
the place where your glory abides.*
PSALM 26:8 NRSV

Your home is so important to you. It's the place where you can be
yourself. It's the place where you feel safe, relaxed, and happy. As a
mother, you enjoy taking care of your home. It's where you raise

your children. There is no place
like home.

You have another home,
too. God's home is also your
home and your children's home.
You go to God's house whenever you go to church.

God's home is bigger than
any church—God's home is anywhere God lives. God's home is as
big as heaven and as small as the most secret, inner room in your
heart. You love the house in which God dwells—whether it's your
local church or the depths of your own heart. You can go home to
visit God and enjoy his glory any time you like. For God's house is
all around you, above you, and deep inside you.

You can be at home with God any time you like.

One thing I have asked from the
LORD, that I shall seek:
that I may dwell in the house of
the LORD all the days of my life,
to behold the beauty of the LORD
and to meditate in His temple.

PSALM 27:4 NASB

God's Peace

The LORD is my light and my salvation; whom
shall I fear? The LORD is the strength of my
life; of whom shall I be afraid?

PSALM 27:1 KJV

Family, friends, and media have told you how challenging a mother's job is. "Say good-bye to sleep and privacy." "Just wait till they're teenagers." "Paying for college takes a lot of sacrifices." "Your life just isn't your own until they graduate." As if you didn't know. But so what? You know that motherhood is the toughest job you'll ever love—challenges included.

With God on your side, you can do anything. There is nothing and no one to be afraid of. With God in your corner as you raise and love your children, certainly no challenge is too complicated, no obstacle is insurmountable, and no problem is insoluble. Your God is the stronghold of your life and the lives of your children. Sure, being a mother can be a tough job—but it's also an infinitely joyful job when you trust God to work all things for good.

God is your light and salvation.
With God, all things are possible.

*H*e alone is my rock and
my savior—my stronghold.
I cannot be severely shaken.

PSALM 62:2 GOD'S WORD

God Is Good

Give thanks to the LORD because he is good.
His love continues forever.
PSALM 136:1 NCV

It's all good. You watch your children grow and learn and love and laugh. You enjoy motherhood with all of its blessings, rewards,

and challenges. You wouldn't change places with anyone else in the world. Being a mother is all good.

The source of all goodness, of course, is God, and God can't wait to pour his goodness on you—every moment of every day. You don't have to wait to get to heaven to experience how good God is. Every day you pick up the kids at school, help them with their homework, or watch them play in the backyard, you enjoy the goodness of God. Every time you wipe away a tear, hold a little hand to cross the street, or wave good-bye as they go off to summer camp, you touch God's goodness.

You are a mother. You are blessed. For you have seen the goodness of the Lord in the land of the living.

You believe that you shall see the
goodness of the Lord today.

I will praise you forever for what you have done; in your name I will hope, for your name is good. I will praise you in the presence of your saints.

PSALM 52:9 NIV

The Power of Thanks

Sing praises to the LORD, O you his faithful ones,
and give thanks to his holy name.

PSALM 30:4 NRSV

"Thanks, Mom," she says after you've talked with her late into the night about her first prom. "Thanks, Mom," he says, hugging you, his college diploma gripped in his right hand. You don't do it for the thanks, of course. You do it out of love. You'd give them the whole world if you could, for love alone, but hearing their thanks is awfully nice. Like icing on a cake.

Imagine how God feels when you say, "Thank you, God." Your thanks go right to God's heart. It's not just the big things in life you're grateful for. The smaller the blessing, the more powerful your thanks to God, who blesses you. You take nothing in your world for granted, for all good gifts come from God. God doesn't do it for the thanks, of course. He does it out of love but, oh, how he loves to hear his children thank him.

Today you say, "Thank you, God,"
for your world and all that is in it.

Let everyone give thanks to you, O God. Let everyone give thanks to you.

PSALM 67:3 GOD'S WORD

In God's Hand

Into your hands I commit my spirit;
redeem me, O LORD, the God of truth.
PSALM 31:5 NIV

*J*ust getting out the door any weekday morning can be a challenge. Get the kids up and dressed. Make lunches. Take them to school. It's another busy morning. With all that you have to do as a mom this day, it's easy to forget God.

As you herd everybody out the door for another day of school and work, pray a simple prayer to help yourself remember who's really in control: *Into your hands I commit my spirit.*

This simple prayer says to God, *You, O Lord, are in control of my life—not me.* It says to God, *I want to be with you every moment of every day no matter how crazy today gets.* It says to God, *No matter what happens today, you bring goodness to all who love you.* It says to God, *I love you.* Is there any better way for you as a busy mom to begin your day?

O God, hear this simple prayer: Into
your hands I commit my spirit.

I follow close behind you; your strong right hand holds me securely.

PSALM 63:8 NLT

The Joy of Forgiveness

Count yourself lucky, how happy you must be—
you get a fresh start, your slate's wiped clean.
PSALM 32:1 THE MESSAGE

Sometimes you make mistakes. Sometimes you act without thinking. Sometimes you may not do your best, but your heart is in the right place, and your intentions are full of love.

Thank God that you can go to God for forgiveness. Forgiveness springs from deep love. When you seek God's forgiveness, God looks deep into your heart and sees the love you have there—and God forgives you. The joy of forgiveness is the ability to start over again. The joy of forgiveness is to love deeper and better than before. The joy of forgiveness is being able to forgive your children and family as God has forgiven you. The joy of forgiveness is freedom from being stuck in the past and the freedom to love again.

The joy of God's forgiveness is available to you any time, day or night. Your God waits with open, loving arms for you to experience the joy of forgiveness.

You can ask for God's forgiveness any time you need to.

As far as the east is from the west—that is how far he has removed our rebellious acts from himself.

PSALM 103:12 GOD'S WORD

A Mother's Blessing

I bless God every chance I get; my lungs expand with
his praise. I live and breathe GOD; if things aren't
going well, hear this and be happy: Join me in
spreading the news; together let's get the word out.

PSALM 34:1–3 THE MESSAGE

You have experienced God's blessing. Of all the blessings of this
life, none are greater than your children.
Your children are God's living, breathing,
walking blessings. Your children are
God's love for you clothed in flesh.

Yes, God has greatly blessed you, but
what is it to bless God? What could God
possibly want or need from you? God
wants you to love him. You clothe your
love for God every time you praise and bless him. Your blessings and
praise of God put legs on your love for God-—your words run
straight to God's ears and into God's heart. Blessing God goes
beyond thanking God—blessing God is telling God of your wild and
boundless love for him. Because you are a mother and you are
deeply, profoundly blessed by God with your children, you naturally
return God's blessing by singing God's praises with your lips, with
your heart, with your very life.

You will bless the Lord all day long; his
praise will always be in your mouth.

We will celebrate and praise
you, LORD! You are good to us,
and your love never fails.

PSALM 106:1 CEV

God's Faithfulness

God's love is meteoric, his loyalty astronomic,
his purpose titanic, his verdicts oceanic.
PSALM 36:5 THE MESSAGE

As a mother, you know that God's greatest gift is faithfulness. You know that no matter what your children do, you will never leave or abandon them. Because you are a mother, you stand by your children, come what may. Even when your children grow up and have families of their own, your love never stops. You are faithful to your children throughout your life.

No matter what you do in your life, God will never leave you. God is always faithful. God walks with you when times are good; God sustains you when times are tough. God holds you in the palm of his hand, regardless of how good you are. God's love for you is so deep and wide that God journeys beside you, holding your hand, leading the way through thick and thin. God loves you with a mother's kind of love. God's faithfulness will never let you go.

God's faithfulness toward you is as vast as
the heavens and as deep as the sea.

How precious is your steadfast love,
O God! All people may take refuge in
the shadow of your wings.

PSALM 36:7 NRSV

Teach Your Children

I have been young, and now am old, yet I have not seen the righteous forsaken or their children begging bread.
PSALM 37:25 NRSV

Most mothers are naturally generous people, and as a mother, you are probably very good at giving. One of the most precious gifts you can give your children is a generous and open spirit. With a generous spirit, children develop into secure and confident adults who are able to give to others out of their strength and their love. People who learn generosity as children are blessings to their parents.

God wants you to teach your children about generosity. God assures you that when you give liberally, your children become blessings. God returns generosity to you a hundredfold as your children put into practice what they learn from you—to give of themselves, their resources, their love, and their time unconditionally and without fear. You have the pleasure of watching your children grow into generous spirits who will one day teach their children the beauty and quiet spiritual reward of generosity.

God wants you to teach your children to give generously today.

I will instruct you and
train you in the way you
shall go; I will counsel
you with My eye on you.

Psalm 32:8 MLB

Waiting for God

Be still before the LORD, and wait patiently for him; do not fret over those who prosper in their way, over those who carry out evil devices.

PSALM 37:7 NRSV

Mothers know a lot about patience. Your children teach you. You must be patient when your children are learning how to do things for themselves, whether it's learning to tie their shoes or finishing a complicated set of math problems on a school night. You want them to hurry up—there's so much else to do! Patience tells you that you have to let them learn at their own speed, if they are to learn well.

There's another kind of patience you know about too. God teaches you. There are no hard and fast rules to being a good mother. God wants you to learn as you go at your own speed. Sometimes you may want to be like other moms in the neighborhood who seem to have it all together, but God isn't finished with you yet. You must patiently wait for God to help you become a good mom day by day.

Have patience. God isn't finished with you yet.

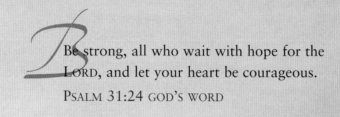

Be strong, all who wait with hope for the LORD, and let your heart be courageous.

PSALM 31:24 GOD'S WORD

God's Law in a Mother's Heart

I delight to do your will, O my God;
your law is within my heart.

PSALM 40:8 NRSV

*I*t takes a lot of physical energy to be a mom these days. Just keeping up with your children is a full-time job, and some moms have full-time jobs working for somebody else as well. It also takes a lot of spiritual and emotional energy to be a good mother. You give your heart to your kids every moment of every day.

God renews your heart and gives you the emotional and spiritual strength you need so you can be there for your children 100 percent. When you keep God's law, God's Word, in your hearts, you find the energy you need for motherhood. Reading the Bible and remembering favorite verses is a tremendous spiritual boost in the midst of a demanding day filled with kids and work. Keeping and meditating on God's law in your heart gives you a tranquil spirit—a spirit that can help you manage anything.

*Y*ou have the energy you need for today because
you keep God's law in your heart.

Inspiring Words FROM THE PSALMS

The law of the LORD is perfect, convert-
ing the soul: the testimony of the LORD
is sure, making wise the simple.

PSALM 19:7 KJV

Praiseworthy

*Then let me go to the altar of God, to
God my highest joy, and I will give thanks
to you on the lyre, O God, my God.*

PSALM 43:4 GOD'S WORD

Mother's Day is fun. A lot of what you do is taken for granted by your children, but on Mother's Day you become worthy of praise! You are showered with gifts; you are taken out to brunch or dinner. Your church recognizes and honors you on Mother's Day. It's a kick.

It's easy sometimes to take all God does for you for granted. The Bible tells you that God is worthy of praise. The next time you have a little time for yourself, you might try this: Proclaim God's Day! Sing God's praises. Or play music on the stereo that's pleasing to God. Bring gifts of flowers and herbs from the garden inside and dedicate them to God. Make a list of blessings and thank God for each one. Let God's Day be a day of joy, a day of praise, a day of song. Have fun.

*Today is God's Day. Today you can sing
and dance and love God.*

My praise shall be of thee in the great congregation: I will pay my vows before them that fear him.

PSALM 22:25 KJV

Simple Joy

O clap your hands, all peoples;
shout to God with the voice of joy.
PSALM 47:1 NASB

Think for a minute about the simple joys of motherhood. Baby pulls herself up using the sofa and takes her first steps across the carpet. She floats elegantly down the staircase in her first prom dress. Gravely and proudly, she accepts her college diploma from the dean. Looking tired but blissful in a hospital room, she adjusts the blanket that holds her own baby—the first grandchild. Nothing—no other experience, no amount of money—can compare to the simple joys your children bring you.

For nurturing and watching your children grow up, you are truly thankful—and you are full of praise to your Creator, who makes all of these moments of joy possible. You want to clap your hands. You want to shout for joy. God, looking down from heaven on your simple joy, rejoices with you—he claps and sings and shouts, and all the angels in heaven join in joy.

Clap and shout for joy. God touches your life.

Great is the LORD and greatly to be praised in the city of our God. His holy mountain, beautiful in elevation, is the joy of all the earth, Mount Zion, in the far north, the city of the great King.

PSALM 48:1–2 NRSV

A Mother Knows

My mouth shall speak wisdom,
and the meditation of my heart shall give understanding.
PSALM 49:3 NKJV

It's common for a new, first-time mother to fear that she won't know what to do or how to care for her baby when he is born. Prior to birth, a soon-to-be new mother spends anxious months reading up on baby care and parenting. And then the day comes—you are a mother. As the new baby nestles quietly in your arms after birth, your "mother's instinct" kicks in, along with joy, and you just know it's all going to be all right.

So it is in the life of faith. You don't need to know all the answers beforehand. You need only to meditate in your heart on the love of God day by day. God will give you the understanding and the knowledge you need to journey with him. The understanding that God gives is like a mother's instinct—you'll know what to do; and it'll be all right.

As you meditate on God's love in your heart,
you'll know what God wants from you.

I remember my song in the
night and reflect on it.

PSALM 77:6 GOD'S WORD

Trusting God

Nevertheless I am continually with you;
you hold my right hand.
PSALM 73:23 NRSV

Y ou have held the hands of your small children while crossing a busy street. Hands firmly in yours, your children carefully step off the curb and follow at your side. Your children are oblivious to the traffic and the danger of missteps. They are content to go with you where you lead, completely trusting you without a thought or understanding of the peril involved in crossing any street.

God desires that same kind of trust from you. God promises to hold your hand no matter what. With your hand firmly in his, God asks that you trust him, that you follow him no matter where he leads you. You don't worry or fret or whine. You know God's right hand holds your small, frail human hand. You follow at his side without a care in the world, knowing only that God's love has ahold of you and your children.

You can walk confidently through the day
because God holds your hands.

I will sing of the LORD's great love forever; with my mouth I will make your faithfulness known through all generations. I will declare that your love stands firm forever, that you established your faithfulness in heaven itself.

PSALM 89:1–2 NIV

God's Purpose for You

*We are your people, the sheep of your flock. We will
thank you always; forever and ever we will praise you.*
PSALM 79:13 NCV

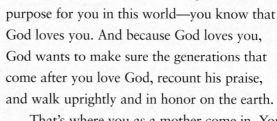

God's ways are mysterious, but you know something about his
purpose for you in this world—you know that
God loves you. And because God loves you,
God wants to make sure the generations that
come after you love God, recount his praise,
and walk uprightly and in honor on the earth.

That's where you as a mother come in. You
are part of God's divine purpose to make sure
that generation follows generation to give God
thanks and praise. One of the most important jobs of motherhood is
to train and teach and raise your children to love God, to give God
thanks and praise, and to grow into honorable adulthood, respecting
others and doing good for those less fortunate. What an awesome
and powerful purpose! Being a mother is a holy calling from God.
You can be both proud and humbled to carry out God's purpose.

*You are a mother. Today you carry out
God's purpose for you.*

In order that the succeeding generation might know, that the children still to be born might arise and recount it to their sons, so as to put their confidence in God and not forget God's works, but to keep His commandments.

PSALM 78:6–7 MLB

A Mother's Place

Even the sparrow has found a home, and the swallow a nest
for herself, where she may have her young—a place near your
altar, O LORD Almighty, my King and my God.

PSALM 84:3 NIV

Maybe it's because you are a mom that you love your home so much. You work to make your home a comfortable, clean place for your family. You browse women's magazines looking for decorating ideas; you try out the latest cleaning products; you install appliances to help you keep your home neat and tidy; you may put in long hours in the garden to add to the beauty of your home. There is truly no place like home. So you spend a lot of time—and money—making sure your home is the best place can be.

Home is also a sanctuary. It is where you dwell with God every day. It may not be a very quiet place, filled with children and pets and all. Yet it is a place of peace, a place of wholeness. It is a place where your family and you can retreat from a fragmented and demanding world to find God.

You are a mother, a keeper of God's
sanctuary, your home.

How blessed are those
who dwell in Your
house! They are ever
praising You.

PSALM 84:4 NASB

The Power of Self-Control

The LORD God is a sun and shield; the LORD
bestows favor and honor; no good thing does he
withhold from those whose walk is blameless.

PSALM 84:11 NIV

Raising children usually means exercising some self-control over your lifestyle. Remember what it was like before the children started arriving? Vacations at grown-up destinations instead of theme parks; driving a sporty two-door instead of a minivan; enjoying a night on the town with friends without having to budget for a baby-sitter; going to a restaurant with cloth napkins instead of to a fast-food counter that packages happy toys with the meals.

Self-control for the sake of your children is more than a lifestyle choice. It is making sure you live a life that is pleasing to God. Such self-control is not hard—for God gives good things to those who walk uprightly. The benefit to your children is immense—they learn to live like Mom, who is generous, grateful, and full of love for God and his ways.

The power of self-control is the love of God, who gives all
good things to those who live life with honor and integrity.

Create in me a clean heart, O God.
Renew a right spirit within me.

PSALM 51:10 NLT

Compassionate Motherhood

Make glad the soul of Your servant,
for to You, O Lord, I lift up my soul.
For You, Lord, are good, and ready to forgive,
and abundant in lovingkindness to all who call upon You.

PSALM 86:4–5 NASB

A mother is compassionate by nature. One of the things you do as a mom is to cheer up your children when they have had a bad day or are frightened or are otherwise sad. You wipe away the tears and try to divert their attention by helping them to do something happy—maybe a tea party in the backyard or a bike ride around the block or an impromptu fort from a blanket thrown over the dining table.

Your God is compassionate too. Whenever you are frightened or otherwise sad, you can go to God and ask him to gladden your heart. You know that God is loving and good and forgiving—and that God can't wait to help you into happier times. When you go to God like a child who needs cheering up, God will have compassion on you. You can be assured that his goodness and his love will make you happy again.

God will gladden your soul and
restore you to happiness.

My lips will praise you
because your mercy is
better than life itself.

PSALM 63:3 GOD'S WORD

Gratitude —A Way of Life

I will praise You, O Lord my God, with all my
heart, and I will glorify Your name forevermore.
PSALM 86:12 NKJV

You teach your children to say "please" and "thank you." Saying "please" and "thank you" is more than just being polite. Saying "please" and "thank you" expresses a civilized way of interacting with others in life. Saying "please" and "thank you" puts a little oil on the cogs and gears that make day-to-day social life possible. Those simple but polite words help you all to get along.

Saying "thank you" to God is a way of life. In fact, a life lived in gratitude to God is a life lived in faith. Saying "thank you" to God for his blessings, for his watch over you and your children, and for his love, mercy, and grace keeps your relationship with God growing. Being grateful to God keeps you from taking God and his work in your life for granted. Saying "Thank you, God" tells God you want him in your life.

You give thanks to God today
with your whole heart.

It is good to give thanks to the LORD, to sing praises to your name, O Most High; to declare your steadfast love in the morning, and your faithfulness by night.

PSALM 92:1–2 NRSV

Promise Keeping

Praise the LORD, you his angels, you mighty ones
who do his bidding, who obey his word.

PSALM 103:20 NIV

Every mother knows how important promises are to children.
When children make promises to each other, their promises are
sealed with childhood vows to keep them,
including chants to "stick a needle in my
eye" or spit and handshakes. A child's world
stands or falls depending on how well promises are kept. A broken promise brings big
tears and wailing condemnation—"but you
promised!"

A mother is a promise keeper. You promise God to keep his words—to love and
respect one another, to show mercy and forgiveness, to be a woman
of faith. You promise your children to be the best mother you can
be, to love them and take care of them and raise them well. Your
children watch you keeping your promise to God, and they grow up
to be promise keepers too. They become people of faith, who love
and respect one another, who promise to keep God's words.

You will tell of God's faithfulness and
promise to keep God's words.

*Y*ou are my inheritance, O LORD.
I promised to hold on to your words.

PSALM 119:57 GOD'S WORD

Guardian Angels

*He will command his angels concerning
you to guard you in all your ways.*
PSALM 91:11 NRSV

When your children leave you, even for just a little while, you may
stand at the front door waving good-bye and
praying a silent prayer. You pray that God's
angels will defend and protect your children.
You pray that your children's angels will
hover over them and journey with them and
bring them safely home.

You have a guardian angel too. Because
you are a mother and your work is important to God, he sends his angels to guard
you in all your ways. You know that when you've had a particularly
tough day with the kids or when you need extra energy to help them
do their homework, your guardian angel will hover over you, whis-
pering encouragement and God's love to your heart. So the next time
you stand at the front door waving good-bye, know that your own
guardian angel watches over you and waits with you until your children return safely home.

*Today God sends his guardian angels to
take care of your children and you.*

God says, "I will save those who love me and will protect those who acknowledge me as LORD. When they call on me, I will answer them; when they are in trouble, I will be with them.

PSALM 91:14–15 GNT

A Mother Is an Optimist

You, O LORD, have made me glad by what You have done, I will sing for joy at the works of Your hands.

PSALM 92:4 NASB

A mother is a natural optimist. You look down at the baby in your arms and think, *Maybe he's a future president of the United States.* Or, *Maybe she'll be a nuclear physicist.* Or, *Maybe she'll follow in her father's footsteps.* Your positive dreams for your children make you an optimist, and that optimism helps give you the energy and foresight you need to make sure that your children's future is bright. You are full of hope for the exciting fulfillment of your dreams.

You are made glad by the works of God's hands, your children. As you hold God's work in your arms, you see a bundle full of promise. Your gladness and your hope are so great that sometimes you feel as if your soul could burst with joy. Being filled with hope and promise such as this, who can keep from singing praises to God?

You have only to look in your children's eyes to see that today is filled with hope and promise.

*O*ur LORD and our God,
you give these blessings
to all who worship you.

PSALM 144:15 CEV

The Beauty of Worship

O come, let us worship and bow down: let us kneel
before the LORD our maker. For he is our God; and we
are the people of his pasture, and the sheep of his hand.

PSALM 95:6–7 KJV

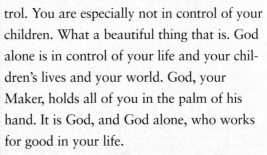

As a mother, you are loving, resourceful, optimistic, and devoted to your children. There is one thing you're not—you are not in control. You are especially not in control of your children. What a beautiful thing that is. God alone is in control of your life and your children's lives and your world. God, your Maker, holds all of you in the palm of his hand. It is God, and God alone, who works for good in your life.

When you worship God, you acknowledge that you are not in control and that you have faith and trust that God is in control of your world. What freedom it is to give up trying to be in charge. What freedom it is to give God the reins and let God do his work. When you worship God, you give up control, and you are free to be a good mother and love your children.

You are not a shepherd. You are
a sheep in God's hand.

I bow before your holy Temple as I worship. I will give thanks to your name for your unfailing love and faithfulness, because your promises are backed by all the honor of your name. When I pray, you answer me; you encourage me by giving me the strength I need.

PSALM 138:2–3 NLT

The Creativity of Motherhood

Sing to the LORD a new song; sing to the LORD, all the earth. Sing to the LORD, praise his name; proclaim his salvation day after day.

PSALM 96:1–2 NIV

As a mother, you are creative. You use your creativity to entertain your children on a rainy day—from finger painting to modeling with clay to improvising hideouts. You may spend hours at the sewing machine to make fun, attractive clothes; you may make countless batches of chocolate-chip cookies—all because you love your children. In fact, you could say that motherhood is one big creative project.

In God's hands, you are an instrument of God's creativity. You are like a musical instrument played by a fine musician who plays songs that are fresh and new and have never been heard before. Through you, God creates and brings something new and unique into the world—your children. Children are like new songs—no two, not even twins, are exactly alike. Each child is a new, distinct, and irreplaceable person. Each child is a new song that God sings.

Sing to the Lord a new song, for you are an instrument in his hands.

You alone created my inner being. You knitted me together inside my mother. I will give thanks to you because I have been so amazingly and miraculously made. Your works are miraculous, and my soul is fully aware of this.

PSALM 139:13–14 GOD'S WORD

Your Children Tell God's Glory

Ascribe to the LORD, O families of the peoples,
ascribe to the LORD glory and strength.
PSALM 96:7 NASB

Your children are your crown and your glory. Not only do you love them deeply, but you're proud of who they are and what they do in the world. Even the family pet is a special source of pride and joy. Your children tell the world a lot about you as a mother—their character and integrity make you look good.

Your children also tell the world a lot about God. A family bound together by the love and grace of God tells the world that God is loving and merciful. A family whose members love and respect each other because of God tells the world that God is strong and good. Not only are your children your own crown and glory, they are the glory of God. Families are God's pride and joy. For through families, God tells the world that he is busy at work in the world.

Your family glorifies God; your children
are jewels in God's crown.

How very good and
pleasant it is when
kindred live together
in unity!

PSALM 133:1 NRSV

A Quiet Morning with God

Light dawns for the righteous,
and joy for the upright in heart.
PSALM 97:11 NRSV

Occasionally you may awake early, well before the alarm goes off. The house is quiet. Time to start getting ready for school and work is still a ways off. Wide awake, you're faced

with a choice—you can toss and turn and fret when sleep won't come, or you can get up and do something useful until sleepiness returns.

Grab a light blanket and a Bible and head for the couch. There in the predawn quiet you can do something truly useful—you can spend a quiet morning with God. You can open the Bible to any page and read until a verse touches your heart. You can reread favorite passages and pray. Sometimes, even at three in the morning, your heart may be full of joy. You can sing quietly to your God, who is the source of all joy. When sleep finally begins to return, you can thank God that you are his child and tiptoe softly back to bed.

Joy comes in the morning for God's children.

I could say, "The darkness will hide me. Let the light around me turn into night." But even the darkness is not dark to you. The night is as light as the day; darkness and light are the same to you.

PSALM 139:11–12 NCV

You Know Who You Are

O Lord, You have searched me and known me.
PSALM 139:1 NKJV

You have probably often looked at your sleeping children and felt awed and humbled. During such moments, you know that this is what life is really all about. You want nothing more than this—to be the mother of this precious gift, your children.

Humility is a spiritual gift. It doesn't mean you walk around putting yourself down or thinking badly of yourself. True humility is knowing who you really are—and thanking God for who you are in this life. Your friends or the people at work may think they know you, but you know who you really are underneath all those other roles—you are a mother, chosen by God to bring your children to life and raise them to love and honor God. Motherhood is a calling that inspires awe—and true humility—in your heart. You can rejoice and thank God that you know who you are.

Motherhood is a humble, beautiful gift of God.

*Y*You know the LORD is God! He created
us, and we belong to him; we are his
people, the sheep in his pasture.

PSALM 100:3 CEV

A Mother Models Integrity

I will sing of lovingkindness and justice,
to You, O LORD, I will sing praises.
PSALM 101:1 NASB

When you are dealing with a person of integrity, you know that what you see is what you get. A person of integrity does what she says she's going to do. A person of integrity has no hidden agendas. A person of integrity lives his beliefs. A person of integrity inspires trust and loyalty in others.

As a mother, you want your children to grow up into people of integrity. As a mother, you model integrity for your children when your behavior is consistent with your faith—when you keep your promises; when you have mercy on those less fortunate; when you generously share your love of God. In other words, you model integrity when you walk the talk. Your children are watching your every move, eager to copy what you do and say. Over the years, they will grow into strong adults who love God and walk with integrity of heart.

The love of God and practice of your faith let you
model integrity for your children.

My eyes will be watching the faithful people in the land so that they may live with me. The person who lives with integrity will serve me.

PSALM 101:6 GOD'S WORD

Your Children's Heritage

The children of Your servants will continue,
and their descendants will be established before You.
PSALM 102:28 NKJV

When you become a grandmother, it's as though all of your dreams have finally come true. It's a different kind of miracle from having your own children. To hold your grandchildren in your arms is to hold a little bit of the future that you will never see. When you're with your grandchildren, you know yourself to be a link in an incredibly long and wonderful family chain. You rejoice and give thanks that God has let you see your children's children.

Your faith is for generations. The trust and belief you have in God are a gift to future generations, who will learn from you the joy of loving God. As a grandmother, you can show your grandchildren God's way. It is your grandchildren who will carry your faith deep into the future for generations to come. In a very real sense, a grandmother's faith is forever.

Your children's heritage, your grandchildren,
are the future in God's hands.

You want me to be completely truthful, so teach me wisdom.

PSALM 51:6 NCV

The Benefits of Believing

Bless the LORD, O my soul, and all that is within me, bless his holy name. Bless the LORD, O my soul, and do not forget all his benefits.

PSALM 103:1–2 NRSV

Though they may be easy to forget during a particularly hectic

day, there are many benefits to motherhood. You get the unparalleled joy of watching your children grow up. You get to play with them as well as take care of them. You get to enjoy the affection of your children when they are little. When they are grown, you get to enjoy them as adults and to receive their love.

There are many benefits to believing in God, too. You get to experience God's mercy and grace when you make mistakes. You get to feel God's love when you look in on your napping children. You get to thank God for giving you all that you need to live and love. You get to worship God, the Creator of your children—and your children's children. You wouldn't trade motherhood or your life of faith for anything in the world.

You will remember all the benefits of believing in God today.

Blessed be the Lord,
who daily loads us with benefits,
the God of our salvation!

PSALM 68:19 NKJV

Mothers and Other Living Things

*O LORD, how manifold are Your works! In wisdom You have made them
all. The earth is full of Your possessions— This great and wide sea, in
which are innumerable teeming things, living things both small and great.*

PSALM 104:24–25 NKJV

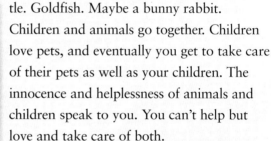

Cats. Dogs. Hamsters. Several frogs over a period of time. A turtle. Goldfish. Maybe a bunny rabbit. Children and animals go together. Children love pets, and eventually you get to take care of their pets as well as your children. The innocence and helplessness of animals and children speak to you. You can't help but love and take care of both.

There's something about being a mother that forms a special connection between the rest of God's creatures and you. Maybe because you bring children into the world, you understand the mother-offspring connection among all creatures. You know the love that God must have for the animals he makes. The connection is creation. Your instinct to love and care for your children—and even their pets—is rooted in your role as a creator with God to bring your children into the world. You rejoice in all God's creatures, great and small.

God loves all the children and animals—and so do you.

Ships sail on it, and Leviathan, which you made, plays in it. All of them look to you to give them their food at the right time. You give it to them, and they gather it up. You open your hand, and they are filled with blessings.

PSALM 104:26–28 GOD'S WORD

A Mother Doesn't Give Up

Seek the LORD, and his strength: seek his face evermore.
Remember his marvellous works that he hath done; his wonders,
and the judgments of his mouth; O ye seed of Abraham his
servant, ye children of Jacob his chosen.

PSALM 105:4-6 KJV

As a mother, you persevere. It's not in your nature to give up when the going gets a little tough. Sure, you've got a lot on your plate—in addition to being a full-time mom, you may have a full-time job, but you manage. You cope. Most of the time, you juggle your life very well—you have to because the happiness and well-being of your children are at stake.

You persevere in another way, too. You are always seeking God and his strength. There's so much that you can't afford not to do. You know that when you are in touch with God, he will give you all you need to be a good mother. God will give you the will to persevere. You know that when you search for God, you find that God is not only looking down on you from heaven, but he is right there walking beside you.

Today you can persevere because you have found God.

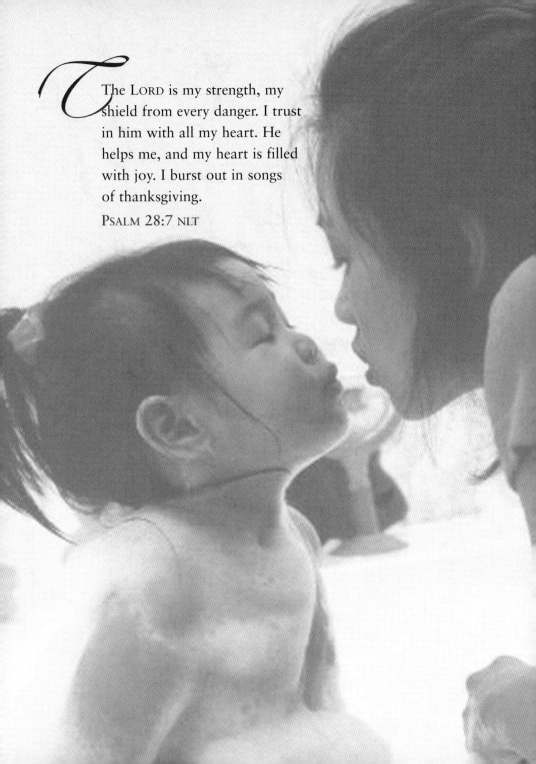

The LORD is my strength, my shield from every danger. I trust in him with all my heart. He helps me, and my heart is filled with joy. I burst out in songs of thanksgiving.

PSALM 28:7 NLT

Love Is Forever

Great is your love, higher than the heavens; your faithfulness reaches to the skies.

PSALM 108:4 NIV

A mother's love is limitless. Your love for your children doesn't stop when they grow up. Instead, your love deepens and grows with them. When your children have children of their own, even more love is born in your heart. Your mother's love is so big it even expands beyond your own family to include friends and neighbors. When you became a mother, God gave you a very big heart.

God's love is forever. God loves you and your children and all that is in your world, his creation. God's love is not limited by time. God pours his love on you all of your days—and well beyond, in heaven. There is no place you can go that God's love can't find you. There is nothing you can do to stop God from loving you. Touched by God's forever love as you are, your heart is so full of faith that it's hard to keep from singing.

Your love is limitless because God loves you forever.

He ransoms me from death
and surrounds me with love
and tender mercies

PSALM 103:4 NLT

A Mother's Comfort

It was you who took me from the womb; you kept me safe
on my mother's breast. On you I was cast from my birth,
and since my mother bore me you have been my God.

PSALM 22:9–10 NRSV

A mother's life is filled with adventure. The adventure begins with the birth of your children. Along the way you love them. You nurse them when they are sick. You help them with their schoolwork. You coach them through Little League, ballet, soccer, or violin lessons. You clean up after them and nag them about finishing everything on their plates. Through all the adventures motherhood brings, God travels with you and watches over you and comforts you.

Suddenly your children graduate, marry, have children of their own. Your love swells with pride. You know they have begun a great adventure. Even though you may shed tears of joy and pride as your children set off on their journeys, you know that God goes with them—to love them as God has loved them from birth—and a mother's heart is comforted.

At the beginning of all great adventures
in life, you can take comfort in how your
God loves you with a mother's love.

When I am afraid, I put my trust in you. O God, I praise your word. I trust in God, so why should I be afraid? What can mere mortals do to me?

PSALM 56:3–4 NLT

The Apple of God's Eye

Guard me as the apple of the eye;
hide me in the shadow of your wings.

PSALM 17:8 NRSV

Motherhood is all about giving. You give your time and love in abundance to raise your children well. You give your energy and keep getting up to go even more. You give because your children are the apples of your eye. How could you possibly give anything less than your whole self?

To keep giving every minute of every day, you need lots of strength. Knowing how much God loves you is the strength that can keep you going. God loves you deeply and faithfully because you are the apple of God's eye, protected under the shadow of God's wing. You are so dear to God; God loves you as his child. God gives you what you need every day so you can give even more to the apples of your eye. Under the shadow of God's wing, you draw strength from which you give.

You are a mother—the apple of God's eye, kept
safe under the shadow of God's wing.

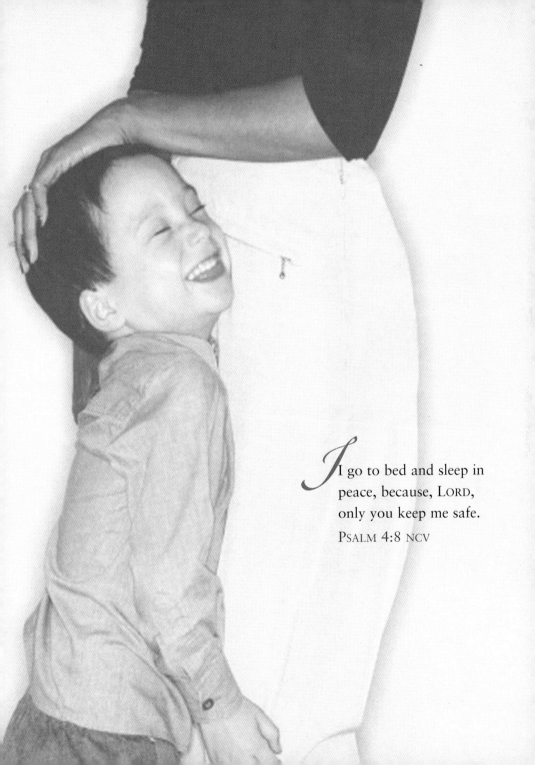

I go to bed and sleep in peace, because, LORD, only you keep me safe.

PSALM 4:8 NCV

Time for God

As a deer longs for flowing streams, so my soul longs for you,
O God. My soul thirsts for God, for the living God.

PSALM 42:1–2 NRSV

You are a very busy person. Your job as a mother is nonstop. You have carpools to drive. Scraped knees to bandage. Meals to cook. Clothes to wash. Homework to oversee. A lot is crammed into your day—usually at the beginning and the end of a busy day.

To keep going—and loving—at such a fast clip, you need to replenish your own thirsty soul. You need time with God, even if it's only a stolen moment or two on the run. Simply thinking about God, who loves you deeply, can quench your thirst for a while. Or thanking God for the love of children and home can keep you going when you're dashing off to the next thing. If your mother's faith is to stay strong, a drink from the heavenly fountain is necessary to sustain and nurture you in all you do.

Today may be busy, but you can take a moment to
drink from God's flowing streams.

The LORD shows his true love every day. At night I have a song, and I pray to my living God.

PSALM 42:8 NCV

Inspiring Words
SERIES

This and other books in the Inspiring Words
series are available from your local bookstore.

Inspiring Words from the Psalms

Inspiring Words from the Psalms for Mothers

Inspiring Words from the Psalms for Women

Inspiring Words from the Psalms for Friends

Blue Sky Ink
Brentwood, Tennessee